SIAMESE FIGHTING FISH

PHOTO BY R. CABRIOL.

This magnificent blue betta has huge, colorful finnage. His tail is especially unique. The strain is called the *Delta Doubletail.*

By
Gene Wolfsheimer

Updated and edited by the staff of
Tropical Fish Hobbyist Magazine.

ABOUT THIS BOOK

Originally published by Pet Library, further editions of the book were not possible due to the untimely death of the author, Gene Wolfsheimer. Long considered as the ultimate booklet for starting hobbyists of *Betta splendens,* the Siamese Fighting Fish, the opportunity finally arose to re-issue the book with completely new illustrations of modern Betta varieties and some textual modifications. The staff of *Tropical Fish Hobbyist Magazine* worked diligently to preserve the flavor of Mr. Wolfsheimer's dedicated work. Not only was Mr. Wolfsheimer the first photographer of an albino Siamese Fighting Fish, but he was also the first person to photograph a spawning of the Discus, *Symphysodon aequifasciatus axelrodi.*

© T.F.H. Publications, Inc.

Distributed in the UNITED STATES to the Pet Trade by T.F.H. Publications, Inc., 1 TFH Plaza, Neptune City, NJ 07753; on the Internet at www.tfh.com; in CANADA by Rolf C. Hagen Inc., 3225 Sartelon St., Montreal, Quebec H4R 1E8; Pet Trade by H & L Pet Supplies Inc., 27 Kingston Crescent, Kitchener, Ontario N2B 2T6; in ENGLAND by T.F.H. Publications, PO Box 74, Havant PO9 5TT; in AUSTRALIA AND THE SOUTH PACIFIC by T.F.H. (Australia), Pty. Ltd., Box 149, Brookvale 2100 N.S.W., Australia; in NEW ZEALAND by Brooklands Aquarium Ltd., 5 McGiven Drive, New Plymouth, RD1 New Zealand; in SOUTH AFRICA by Rolf C. Hagen S.A. (PTY.) LTD., P.O. Box 201199, Durban North 4016, South Africa; in JAPAN by T.F.H. Publications, Japan—Jiro Tsuda, 10-12-3 Ohjidai, Sakura, Chiba 285, Japan. Published by T.F.H. Publications, Inc.
MANUFACTURED IN THE
UNITED STATES OF AMERICA
BY T.F.H. PUBLICATIONS, INC.

CONTENTS

INTRODUCTION

If ever a fish has enlivened the imagination, amazed its beholders, thrilled its audience, and surpassed all other fishes in popularity, it is the Siamese fighting fish, *Betta splendens.* There is little doubt that today's wide fascination with the fishkeeping hobby has been aided and abetted (pronounced "a-betta'd") by this most unique of tropical fishes.

The betta can live comfortably in only enough water to cover it. The betta's brother is apparently his worst enemy. His colors are those of the rainbow. He builds a nest to harbor his offspring and gives them vigilant care. And yet, in comparison with other species, the betta's needs are little, his resistance to illness great. In fact, everything about him is pleasantly gratifying.

Is it any wonder then that the betta attracted the author some fifty years ago, and that it was the first egglaying fish he ever spawned? This spawning took place in a two-gallon aquarium on a kitchen window sill, heated by a green light bulb, partially submerged.

An old style red betta male building his bubble nest.

PHOTO BY HANS JOACHIM RICHTER.

HISTORICAL DATA

Interest in the betta, particularly in its fighting qualities, has lasted for more than 150 years. In its native land, the Siamese were as much aroused by fish fights as their neighbors, the Malaysians, were by cock fights. The fish selected for the aquatic fighting "rings" were chosen for their pugnacious attitude. They were short-finned, streamlined, tenacious creatures bent on dispatching their adversaries quickly.

PHOTO BY HANS JOACHIM RICHTER.

A wild-type Siamese fighting fish.

The Siamese wagered heavily on the outcomes of these battles. Sometimes they even wagered themselves and their families. And because such fights had to be licensed, the King of Siam collected on them as well.

These fighters bore little resemblance to today's bettas with their streamlined beauty, surpassing with their flowing fins and blatant color most of the other tropical aquarium fishes. The wild bettas give little hint of this glory. They are found in ponds, ditches, rice paddies, and sluggish little streams in Thailand and Malaysia. They are nondescript creatures, a dirty greenish brown color. How they found their way into the hearts of today's hobbyists is an interesting story.

In 1849, the time of the California gold rush, Theodor Cantor, a doctor in the Bengal Medical Service, published an article on a fish he called *Macropodus pugnax, var.* He was in error. He had confused his fish with a closely related species which had already been given that name. It was not until 1909 that C. Tate Regan, re-examining the situation, pointed out that *pugnax* was already a valid species. Since Cantor's Siamese fighting fish had no scientific name, Regan described it as *Betta splendens.*

Legend has it that the "Bettah" were a warrior-like tribe of people.

History states that the King of Siam, in 1840, presented

several of his prized fighting fish to a friend of Theodor Cantor. He, in turn, gave them to Dr. Cantor, whose description pictures them thus:

The head is deep greenish olive; the abdomen blood red with the scales edged with black; the body with three black horizontal lines; the dorsal fin silvery greenish brown crossed with wavy black lines; the caudal fin rays a bright blood red edged with black; the caudal fin membranes golden green; the anal fin membranes a bright blood red shading into silvery green to blue; the anal fin rays are black; ventral fin membranes bright red to black; ventral fin rays black, and even the iris in the eye was described as being a pale reddish golden with bluish-black spot in the center of the lower half.

Cantor noted that both the colors and fin lengths varied among specimens. He also commented on the remarkable change that occurred when a relaxed dull-hued fish suddenly, at the prospect of a contest, transformed itself into a fighter of scintillating beauty.

The famed German aquarists, Arnold and Ahl, stated that the first living fighters were introduced into Germany in 1896. Even then, they described their imports as variable in color and short of fin. This same species did not arrive in the United States until 1910.

William T. Innes, the late famed American aquarist, states that in the early days of the hobby, the "original" *Betta splendens* had a body of yellowish brown with a few indistinct horizontal lines. At moments of emotional stress, the male darkened and showed metallic green scales. The dorsal was also this color, tipped with red, while the anal fin was red, tipped with blue. The ventrals were then, as they are now, red, tipped with white. Fins were of moderate size and there was a rounded tail to match.

It was not until 1927 that the first brightly-hued, flowing-finned Siamese fighting fish as we know them today arrived in the United States. They were in a shipment consigned to Frank Locke of San Francisco. He noted both dark-bodied and lighter cream-colored variations. Thinking these light-bodied specimens were a new species, he named them *Betta cambodia*. It soon became evident that this particular variant was only another of the many-hued forms of *Betta splendens*.

Dr. Hugh M. Smith, in his magnificent book, *The Freshwater Fishes of Siam or Thailand*, United States National Museum Bulletin No. 188, describes the species *Betta splendens* so thoroughly that present-day writers continue to forage through his pages to complete their own data. It was Smith who made

PHOTO BY DR. HERBERT R. AXELROD.

A lovely strain of long-finned bettas is the Libby Strain shown above. These three males had a fight. One male quickly gave up and hugged the bottom. The other two tore huge chunks out of each other's fins and ate the pieces! The fish in the background that has the middle portion of his tail missing was just attacked by the fish in the foreground. The foreground fish is eating the piece of tail he just ripped off the fish in the rear.

the observation concerning the strain first known as the Cambodian Betta. He thought that the light-bodied fish with the brightly colored fins originated first in French Indochina in about 1900. The Siamese referred to them as "pla kat khmer" or Cambodian biting fish.

Today, whether they be biters or fighters, alert or sulky, brightly colored or dully hued, they always are identified and readily command attention. "There they are," someone will say, "Those are the Siamese fighting fish." No other comment is necessary. The Betta is very well known.

A long-finned Cambodia-type male. This is the same species, *Betta splendens* as fish of different colors. There are, however, other species of betta. As a matter of fact there are more than a dozen species of *Betta*, most of which do not build bubblenests but are mouth-brooders and the eggs hatch in one of their parents mouths. Dr. Herbert R. Axelrod suggested in 1963 that the genus should be split into those which are mouth brooders and those which are bubblenest builders.

PHOTO BY HANS JOACHIM RICHTER.

PHYSIOLOGICA

The fighting fish, *Betta splendens*, can be found not only in Thailand, but in Malaysia and parts of China and Vietnam. Its native habitats are the flooded rice paddies, quiet, swampy pools, and, on occasion, slowly-moving streams.

We do not mean to imply, however, that the betta we know is native to these waters. Our long-finned, magnificently colored bettas are the product of selective breeding. The native betta hardly ever attains the size of our prize-winning fighters who sometimes exceed five inches in length, tails included. The native male rarely reaches half this size.

Female bettas occasionally attain the body length of the males. They are even greater in girth when full of eggs. However, the females never develop long and pointed fins. Theirs remain short. They are made even shorter by the male during breeding.

The author, at times, had

PHOTO BY HANS JOACHIM RICHTER.

This blue female betta, bulging with eggs, indicates her readiness to spawn by positioning herself under the bubble nest.

maintained a strain of bettas in which the females often carried such exceptional fins (for their sex) that they were mistaken for males. The author also admits to having attempted to breed one of these females, thinking she was a male, to another female. The misidentification occurred because this presumed "male" blew a beautiful bubblenest. Which goes to show that the female betta does, on rare occasion, take on the nest-manufacturing job usually assumed by the male.

Bettas belong to the Belontiidae family. These fish

In Siam (Thailand) two males are put into adjacent jars to prepare them for eventual combat.

PHOTO BY SOMPHONGS LEKAREE.

are noted for their ability to breathe atmospheric air directly from the surface. This is done through an accessory respiratory organ called the labyrinth. This structure is located in the gill chamber alongside and above their normal gills. Atmospheric air gulped in at the surface is forced into the labyrinth organ. This organ is composed of bony plates covered by a membrane through which flows venous blood. By gaseous exchange, passing through the labyrinth organ, the oxygen content is removed to pass immediately into the blood stream. Then the used air is expelled.

The anabantoids are capable of normal gill respiration, but it alone cannot satisfy the fish's requirements. If, by chance, it is prevented from surfacing to acquire needed atmospheric air, the fish can suffocate. This is why the betta, like the other anabantoids, can survive in water with extremely poor oxygen content due to pollution or an overabundance of non-anabantoid fishes.

It is this labyrinth organ which gives credibility to

This wild-type female shows her readiness to spawn by the appearance of the white projection from her anal pore.

PHOTO BY HANS JOACHIM RICHTER.

PHOTO BY R. ZUKAL.

A pair of fighting fish, probably with *Betta imbellis* blood from distant crossings with that species. This photo shows the great difference between males and females.

reports of specimens surviving a night in nothing but a wet net, or being found on the floor in a puddle of water not even deep enough to do more than moisten the flopping fish. Over the years, the author has raised many thousands of bettas, each being kept in its individual one-quart glass jar. Bettas have been found lying on the wet floor. They immediately were returned to their glass homes where they sedately carried on as though nothing had happened.

A comparison of the breathing habits between wild and domesticated bettas is interesting. Both can store only small amounts of air in their extra respiratory organ and must make frequent trips to the surface to replenish it. The aquarist sees his pet hovering just below the surface, languidly surveying life. Not so with its wild brother. In their native habitat, where the fish are exposed to such surface dangers as egrets, herons, kingfishers, and other predatory birds and animals, theirs is a quick dash to the surface, a gulp of air, and a downward dive into the depths. In that moment the used air is expelled and a fresh supply taken in.

The fighting instinct

Ounce for ounce, *Betta splendens* is a far tougher adversary than most fishes, but

PHOTO BY H. J. RICHTER.

Two males preparing for combat. The aggressive male will have his gill plates flared to make him look twice as large! The other fish tends to ignore the aggressor until he is bitten for the first time, then he reacts quickly.

this pugnaciousness is aimed at only one species — his own. Some people find this difficult to comprehend. Fish salesmen constantly must reassure them that the betta does not fight anything and everything. In reality, the opposite is true. The betta is so indifferent to most other fishes that there is a feeling among some that a mistake was made when it was called "Fighting Fish."

In a community aquarium, the betta is likely to be picked on. Some fish will nudge it along to get it going. Others find its long fins a good target for an occasional nip. This is why, if it is at all possible, bettas should be separated not only from their brothers but from almost all other fishes as well. Little plastic trap-like tanks can be hung inside an aquarium to house one or two — not together, of course. There also are available especially designed betta aquariums. These are long and narrow with separate compartments.

The betta usually will fight only a male betta. He also will flare up and try to fight his own reflection in a mirror. Experimentation has shown that even a painted wooden dummy crudely carved to resemble a betta will arouse his wrath.

Why do these fish like to fight? No one can explain it. The fighting instinct does not first appear in a fully mature male as one might think. It

first appears in youngsters not more than nine weeks old. As the young fish develop, little mock battles ensue. The fish, not even an inch long, circle each other head to tail with all of their fins extended and mouth open. Each seems to want the other to "knock a chip off his shoulder." Sometimes there is a quick ripping motion and the skirmish is over.

To raise prime show specimens, separate developing males as soon as their sex is identifiable. Their lengthening fins and their "chip on the shoulder" attitude are the first discernible signs. Ripped fins may grow back but they can leave scars.

The scheduled bout

A planned betta match is carried on much as one might assume. The contestants are shown off, each in its own container. During this period, there is furious betting on the outcome. The fighters then are placed together in a small bowl. With bettas bred specifically for fighting, there is little delay. A few moments of sparring around with spread fins and a flaring of the gills which spread like a huge ruff beneath their heads. Often there is head-to-tail circling with a trembling, shimmying movement. Then, like a flash, the first strike is made.

The damage is all done with the mouth and teeth. Over and over the charging continues, accompanied by ripping and tearing. The circling for advantage and the spreading and trembling of the fins never seem to end. And then, slowly, you come to realize that both fish are being denuded of their people believe, fights to the death. The truth is, a death seldom, if ever, occurs. When the battered combatants are separated and their wounds treated by medicating their

PHOTO BY A. ROTH.

Two males during preliminary battle, their fins are torn. The fish with the most damage eventually was the loser. He was taken out of the arena and nursed back to health, only to lose fight after fight.

fins. Often only shreds remain where there was once a dorsal or tail. What seemed like an hour has taken only a few minutes. At the end, one fish refuses to rise up and charge. It lies sulking and damaged. The other fish, no matter how battered, will continue to challenge. He is considered the winner.

Betta fights are not, as many water and they are kept clean and well fed, healing is very quick. After six or eight weeks, only a few battle scars remain. Even the denuded fins are regrown almost completely.

Life span

The domesticated betta is comparatively short-lived. At from eight to ten weeks, it has matured enough for sex to be determined. The author has bred them when they were only twelve weeks old, but he does not recommend it. They are prime for breeding when they are from 12 to 14 months of age, if they have been raised properly. Breeding can be carried on with older specimens, but problems often arise with the older but more temperamental virgin fish. At two years, the betta is beyond its prime. If it lives for more than three years, it is, indeed, an old fish. Although the author frequently has maintained stock for two years or longer, it was for personal reasons. These old fellows, who in their prime did their part in breeding and continuing their strain, deserved to be pastured off and to receive the best he could offer.

An old male about two years old. He is listless, doesn't hold his fins erect and develops a roundness to the top profile of his body.

PHOTO BY HANS JOACHIM RICHTER.

PHOTOS BY TANAKA.

The greatest breeder of modern bettas is Mr. Tanaka in Japan. The names given to betta varieties differs all over the world. These are called variously gold, yellow, Cambodia or pink. The specific varieties are (1) split or double tail; (2) purple male with torn fins; (3) green gold female; (4) young butterfly bettas. Butterfly bettas have clear fins next to the body with color in the outer portions of the fins. This variety was first developed by Orville Tutwiler in Florida in the 1960's.

PHOTOS AND FISH BY TANAKA.

Tanaka bettas. (1)Black variegated gold male with double tail; (2) green gold male; (3) black variegated split tail; (4) blue butterfly female; (5) pair of gold splash (variegated) bettas; (6) young butterfly bettas; (7) short finned variety males starting combat; (8) ideal butterfly golds with black.

CARE AND MAINTENANCE

Food

Food is of utmost importance with the betta. This fish is a meat eater, definitely carnivorous. Those who feel that the same little shaker can of dry food will suffice this fighter are sure to be disappointed. Such food is accepted, but only as a means of survival.

In the betta's home waters, food consists in great part of mosquito larvae and pupae. In its indigenous surroundings where mosquitoes thrive, the betta plays an important part in the control of this pesty insect. Dr. Smith has estimated that the intake of one adult wild fish can exceed ten thousand larvae a year.

The hobbyist seldom has the desire to collect such food in the wild. Even if he did, local health departments do all they can to discourage the growth of mosquitoes. Substitute foods, meat, or, preferably, living foods, should be fed.

Daphnia, commonly referred to as "water fleas," are good occasionally. These can be obtained at certain times of the year by netting them in lakes or ponds, or they can be purchased at a local aquarium shop. *Daphnia* have been popularized as

Frozen foods offer a wide choice for the betta. Frozen cubes are available at your local pet shop that are appealing to carnivorous fishes.

the best of all living foods. Decidedly they are advantageous, because they are usually "bite-size" and, being from fresh water, will stay alive in the aquarium until eaten. However, professional fish-breeders will feed them only a few times a week in quantity.

Daphnia are a tiny chitinous crustacean. They have for the support of their internal organs an exoskeleton or shell. Eaten in quantity for a prolonged period, *Daphnia* tend to have a laxative effect. Because of this, well-conditioned breeding stock often dwindle in robustness.

Worms make excellent food. *Tubifex* can be fed at irregular times; so can whiteworms or chopped earthworms. Worms always should be rinsed thoroughly before feeding and should always be small enough to be swallowed easily.

Bettas are prone to take bites too big to be swallowed. When they do, they usually manage to get the food down or dislodged and reject it. Once in a while, especially when a small betta swallows a large mosquito larva, everything goes down except the large, round, bulbous head. A betta can choke to death if it is not dislodged. If this happens, hold the fish gently in a wet net and use a pair of tweezers.

In most parts of the country, brine shrimp *(Artemia salina)* are available. These tiny crustaceans that inhabit saltwater flats make an ideal food. Rinse them carefully to remove the salt. Do not overfeed. Those uneaten cannot survive very long in fresh water. Most aquarium shops sell these live, frozen and freeze-dried.

There are many other forms of small aquatic life that can be fed to bettas. Whether a crustacean or the larvae of terrestrial insects, they all give what is most desired by the fighter — something moving to snap at.

Only when living foods are

PHOTO COURTESY OF PENN PLAX.

Bettas have subtle colors which may be invisible under normal light. Fluorescent tubes of various sizes are available to fit every reflector and to achieve the color effects you desire.

Eight examples of variegated splash bettas based upon blues and golds. Those bettas which have bands across the top of the body are sometimes referred to as *saddle* bettas.

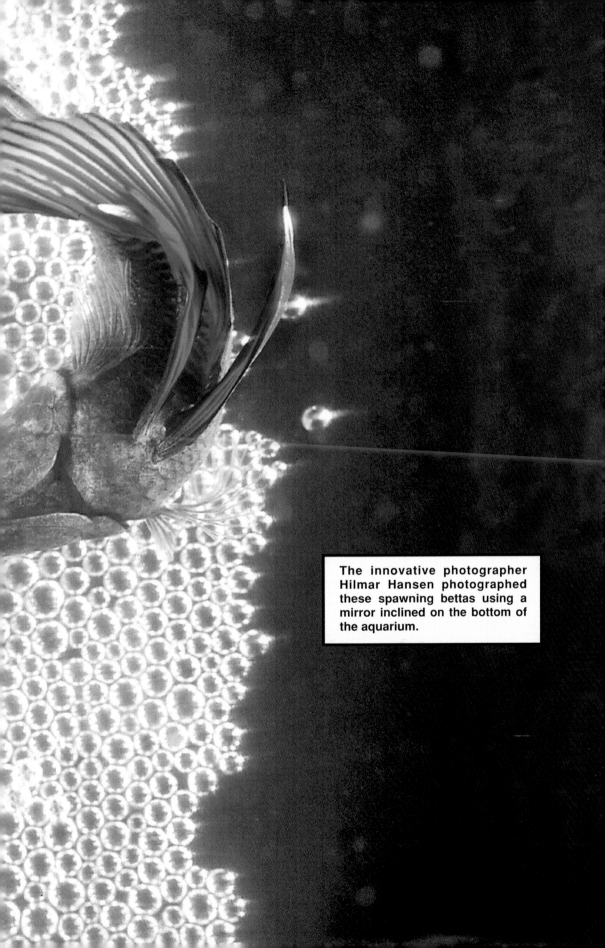

The innovative photographer Hilmar Hansen photographed these spawning bettas using a mirror inclined on the bottom of the aquarium.

unobtainable should substitutes be used. Preferences are as follows. First, scraps and scrapings of various meats and fish. These should be raw and of a size easy to swallow. Red meats should be used with all fibrous matter and fat removed. Second, various frozen foods consisting of aquatic animals usually eaten by fish, such as mosquito larvae, *Daphnia,* and, of course, brine shrimp. Third, commercially-prepared dry fish preparations can be fed. In fact, it is a good idea to feed dry food at least once a week. Choose one whose content is high in protein.

The feeding of baby fish is discussed in the pages on breeding and rearing of young.

Temperature

This plays an important part in maintaining bettas properly. Since these fish come from tropical climes, they should be given the warmth they require. The minimum temperature should be 76°F. Below this, the betta is sluggish. Often his colors are dull. His spirit wanes and so does his appetite. Fins droop, colors diminish, and lassitude leaves him open to hostile attack from other species.

Normal maximum temperature should be below 81°F. Much higher temperatures can be withstood if necessary. Breeding temperatures should be between 80 and 85°F.

Betta keepers can purchase water test kits which enable them to maintain their water well within recommended levels.

Water conditions

The water conditions needed to maintain a betta is far less rigid than that required for many other species. The pH or acidity/alkalinity level varies according to locale. The same is true of the hardness or softness of the water. This is often measured as the "DH" content — German degrees of hardness.

The optimum conditions for the bettas's maintenance and breeding are found in water with a pH of 6.8 - 7.4, and a DH of from 3 - 10. However, he is quick to accept things as they come. He will learn to acclimate to other (if not too extreme) conditions.

It goes without saying that the water should be clear and sweet, and that all vestiges of uneaten or

PHOTOS BY TANAKA.

Tanaka not only breeds bettas for color. He also is interested in the various shapes of their tails. The fish shown here are all Cambodia or golden types. Their tails are all split with different shapes and colors. These tails have no names except for split or double tail.

Betta keepers can purchase water treatment products that enable them to keep their bettas in water at the recommended pH range.

decaying organic matter should be removed. If this is neglected, a general decline and eventually disease can be expected.

Confining a betta in a small jar or allowing it to move freely about in an aquarium is a matter of individual preference. The betta could not care less. Some owners prefer to purchase the small, plastic traps mentioned earlier.

These usually are hung in an upper corner of the aquarium. One or two separated bettas do quite well in this manner.

Those who can maintain bettas in individual glass jars, preferably of a quart or more in size, have the decided advantage of easy cleaning and feeding. In fact, if bettas are bred in captivity, there is no alternative.

Special cleaners are on the market. These do not contain materials dangerous to the fishes and are safe to use around aquaria.

PHOTOS AND FISH BY TANAKA.

(1) Black split tail; (2) black fancy tail (upper lobe smaller than lower lobe); (3) black fancy tail; (4) golden splash split short-tail; (5) veil tail; (6) gold split tail; (7) a magnificent red round tail; (8) a new strain with brown body and red fins with white borders to the rays.

DISEASES

The best disease prevention is a careful maintenance schedule. Keep the water clean, provide adequate heat, and feed a proper diet. If this is done, diseases will be infrequent visitors. Observation is the best precaution. Loss of color and/or appetite, inactivity, droopiness, or discoloration are among the first signs. Others are: abnormal swelling, lesions, external parasitic organisms, fungus, and fin-rotting. Some of these can be treated effectively by remedies already on your shelf; some by obtaining commercial preparations at your nearest aquarium shop.

A fairly common disease is referred to as swim-bladder trouble. Here, an otherwise healthy-looking fish can be seen having difficulty rising to the surface for air. After a battle to reach the top, the life-giving air is inhaled and the betta falls back to the bottom, unable to maintain his buoyancy. There is no specific cure for this problem, although, infrequently, a fish can come out of it spontaneously.

Other outward signs, such as a swollen or dropsical condition, in which the abdomen enlarges, or popped eyes, are not illnesses in themselves. They are symptoms of internal trouble.

A fine treatment on fish diseases is to be found in Dieter Untergasser's *Handbook of Fish Diseases,* (T.F.H. TS-123) available at all pet shops. (They use it themselves!) It is recommended for immediate reference if your bettas start showing any of the above-noted symptoms.

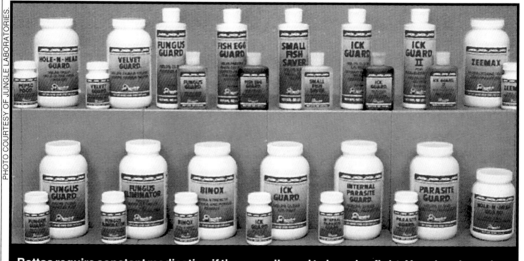

PHOTO COURTESY OF JUNGLE LABORATORIES

Bettas require constant medicating if they are allowed to breed or fight. Your local pet shop has different remedies, preventives and tonics that can be used to treat your bettas.

PHOTOS AND FISH BY TANAKA.

(1) Golden blue doubletail bettas; (2) pin-finned bettas with elongated but frail unpaired fins; (3) black splash male with split tail flaring his gill covers; (4) round tail golden blue splash; (5) round tail golden blues; (6) magnificent red/blue butterfly; (7) a not-so-wonderful butterfly with a round tail; (8) female golden blue splash.

In the 1970's this was the betta of the year. It supposedly was derived from a crossing with *Betta imbellis*. In those years the emphasis was on bright colors and long fins.

PHOTOS AND FISH BY TANAKA.

Tanaka blue bettas showing intense desirable color and varying degrees of bifurcation (split) in their tails.

BREEDING AND REARING OF YOUNG

Breeding bettas, according to the professionals, is not difficult. Novices, however, report varying degrees of success. Perhaps the measure of achievement lies in the participants: the fish, the man — sometimes both.

Young bettas, if brought up should use known strains of fish whose backgrounds will reliably produce the wanted traits. Unfortunately, most novice breeders have little choice because little or nothing is known about their pets' backgrounds. This does not appear to bother the

PHOTO COURTESY OF ROLF. C. HAGEN.

The famed Betta Barracks is an aquarium with compartments for keeping males and females separated until the time comes for them to be together.

properly and not stunted, are capable of being bred when twelve weeks old. Professionals delay any breeding activity until their fish are at least twenty weeks old, or better still, twenty-eight to thirty weeks old. At this age their conformation, coloration, and finnage can be seen at their best.

The breeding stock is of the utmost importance. Breeders novices too much. Most of them just want to "breed fish."

On the other hand, the serious breeder, who has unknown genetic traits to work with, decides where he wants his breeding to go. Then, in subsequent spawnings of progeny after progeny, he slowly approaches his goal. This may be nothing more than obtaining a solidly colored strain. Or it may be as complicated as changing the shape of the body or a fin. In either case, the chosen goal is reached only with selective breeding: with raising the young, with choosing from these the one fish that comes closest to your ideal, and repeating this selective process through successive spawnings until the ideal is reached.

To be successful, it is not enough just to "breed bettas." The novice must be able to rear the young as well. It is here that the beginner sometimes falters.

The pair chosen for breeding obviously must be in the best of condition. Both male and female should have the traits the breeder deems desirable. If he wants to raise red fish, he will breed a pair of bettas truly as red as possible. In this case, knowing the ancestry of the breeding fish would be a help.

When the chosen pair has been selected, they should be kept apart and fed well on a diet of live food, if at all possible. If not, then on top-quality substitutes.

When the male is ready to spawn, he starts to blow bubbles. These appear sometimes as a few

A green male of 1975 standards, starting to prepare his nest. Males can build nests in the hopes of finding a suitable mate.

PHOTO BY HANS JOACHIM RICHTER.

PHOTO BY HANS JOACHIM RICHTER.

This red male has completed his bubble nest. All he needs now is a mate. The female was actually within range of his eyesight in a floating jar.

small "suds" on the surface or as a fully-erected bubblenest — a mound of tiny, white bubbles that spread over from four to six square inches of water and rise to the height of half an inch. This nest is made up of individual gulps of air taken into the buccal cavity where they are given a mucous coating and then expelled. It is a tedious, time-consuming job for the male, but he seldom tires of it. In fact, from his actions it appears to be a highly enjoyable occupation - perhaps in anticipation of the female.

The female betta, ready for breeding, gives fewer, more subtle hints of her ripeness. She should be observed carefully because, if she is not ready when introduced to the male, an unsuccessful spawning will result. (Egg-bound females can release their roe without assistance.)

The female always has played second fiddle to the male. Not blessed with his finnage or coloration, considerably less pretentious, she seldom receives the care given to him. Yet her action at breeding time is of the utmost importance. She should be in prime condition. She should be fairly close in size to the male. Never breed bettas greatly different in size. The female should be alert and active. She should possess a rotund abdomen distended by the ripeness of her eggs. Often, a little, white, bead-like dot will be noticed at her vent. This is the end of the ovipositor or egg-tube. It is a good indication of her readiness for breeding.

The tank setup for betta spawning is simplicity itself. Its size is a matter of preference. The author always has used a three- to five-gallon aquarium. It should be clean and have a full, tight cover. No aeration is needed at breeding time. In fact, still water is essential so that neither the nest nor the eggs it contains will be disturbed. The temperature should be a uniform 82 to 85°F.

The empty breeding tank should be filled to a depth of only four or five inches. A greater depth than this gives added work to the male who must catch both falling eggs and fry which hatch and drift down from the nest. This catching in his mouth is an almost endless procedure. The water used can be either fairly fresh or it can be taken from a

The female comes to join the male under the nest.

PHOTO BY HANS JOACHIM RICHTER.

PHOTO BY ANDRE ROTH.

Some breeders use a floating plastic piece under which the males can build their nests.

clean, healthy aquarium. The breeders are not too particular about this.

A few floating plants can be used as an anchor for the nest. If such plants are not available, a three- to four-inch square of waxed paper can be floated. Males invariably prefer to build their nest beneath something of this sort on the surface.

As we mentioned earlier, prior to introduction into the breeding aquarium, the sexes should be kept apart. There are two ways of accomplishing this. Some divide the aquarium in half with a piece of glass. Others allow the male the run of the aquarium while the female swims in a small, floating jar. She is easily seen, but untouchable.

The male should be allowed to build, or at least start to build, the nest. While doing this, he will carry on a vigorous flirtation with the female. His courtship is an exciting thing to watch. His actions, complete with fin-flaring, tail-batting, and mock entreaties containing masked but obvious threats, are almost unique in fishdom. The confined female does her best to escape her confinement and meet the male's advances.

Finally, the divider is removed and the courtship reaches new heights. Only infrequently does the female respond immediately and follow the male beneath the nest to begin their nuptial embrace. Instead, her timidity increases as the male becomes more audacious. He will strike at her, often making a rough-and-tumble chase out of the courtship. The female should have some place of refuge, such as a small flowerpot lying on its side, or a clump of plants. When the chase reaches such a pitch that the female is endangered (although this sometimes works in reverse, with the male endangered), they again should be separated in the previous manner. This separation and introduction technique safeguards both the breeders from serious injury. Such an injury might cause the discontinuance of the spawning.

Eventually, after one or more separations, the female does agree to follow the male beneath the nest. After a few trials, breeding begins in earnest. They circle each other

The female joins the male under the nest and they body-slap, rubbing against each other under the nest. They often break up the nest with this maneuver.

PHOTO BY HANS JOACHIM RICHTER.

After all the waiting, the spawning embrace under the nest finally occurs. The male fertilizes the eggs as they are expelled by the female.

slowly in a head-to-tail approach. At the propitious moment, the male, moving slowly in a circling motion, enfolds the female in a U-shaped body clutch. They turn slowly upside down in a trembling embrace. Her eggs are released to be fertilized immediately with sperm from the male. When the male releases her, she lies inactive near the surface while little white irregularly-shaped eggs may be seen dropping.

Now the male begins his task of catching the falling eggs in his mouth and carrying them to the nest. He then inspects the bottom of the tank. Any eggs lying about are rescued and returned to the nest as well.

The female normally helps with the egg-catching after she recovers from the embrace. It is here that the success or failure of a spawning often is decided. There are abnormal females who sometimes eat the eggs. To satisfy this craving, they craftily grab those eggs in the nest while the male is elsewhere rescuing others. Fortunately, these egg-eating females are rare. Egg-eating males are even rarer. It does happen, however, that they, too, when left alone to guard the nest, will devour all, or nearly all, of the eggs.

There is more than one

The eggs are in the nest among the floating *Riccia* plants. The male guards them until they hatch.

PHOTO BY HANS JOACHIM RICHTER.

spawning embrace. They are repeated with only short pauses until the female is devoid of eggs. Lengths of spawning vary, depending upon how many eggs the female has. Egg expulsion on each embrace can be as few as one or two, or as many as thirteen to eighteen. An average-size spawning may contain 350-400 eggs. These will take two or three hours to deliver into the nest.

The female should be removed just as soon as the spawning is completed. The male will drive her away from the nest and assume full command of its care. If the female is not removed, she is in serious danger from the male. She should be given clean living quarters with a medication in the water to heal tears and wounds inflicted by the male. If she is fed properly, she should be capable of breeding again in a week or two. For a maximum egg count, keep her from spawning for at least sixteen days.

The male, now in full charge, immediately starts extensive

After the embrace, the female releases some eggs and then floats away unconscious for less than a minute to give the male a chance to collect the eggs, spit them into his bubble nest and to get ready for another embrace.

PHOTO BY HANS JOACHIM RICHTER.

PHOTO BY HANS JOACHIM RICHTER.

Some eggs cling to the female for a short time after fertilization. They drop off as the female recovers and while the male is hunting for the eggs already released.

nest repairs and clustering the eggs together in a fairly compact mass. The treatment of the eggs varies according to the male. Some show a total lack of interest which results in the failure of the spawning. Others are extremely attentive. The nest is not only mended, it is enlarged to magnificent proportions. The eggs are moved and moved again until everything is just right. Finally, completely satisfied with his job, he positions himself beneath the nest and stands his lonely guard.

If the aquarium has been kept covered to prevent air from leaking in and breaking the bubbles, the male's job is an easy one. During this period, he can be fed if desired, but it is not necessary. If not eaten, the food will rot and foul the breeding tank.

At proper breeding temperatures, the betta eggs should hatch in about thirty-six hours. The fry are extremely tiny. They hang vertically with their tails down — a head-in-the-suds position. The male becomes vigilant. He constantly catches and blows back any falling baby.

On the day after hatching, look carefully beneath the nest. Have your eyes follow a line across the surface. The nest will resemble a finely-bristled brush because of all the tails dangling in the water.

On the following day, the fry

PHOTO BY HANS JOACHIM RICHTER.

The male chases the eggs while the female remains stunned under the nest.

PHOTO BY HANS JOACHIM RICHTER.

Spawning was completed a few hours ago. The eggs start swelling as they absorb water. The male keeps blowing them back into the nest as they slowly fall free of a bubble.

PHOTO BY HANS JOACHIM RICHTER.

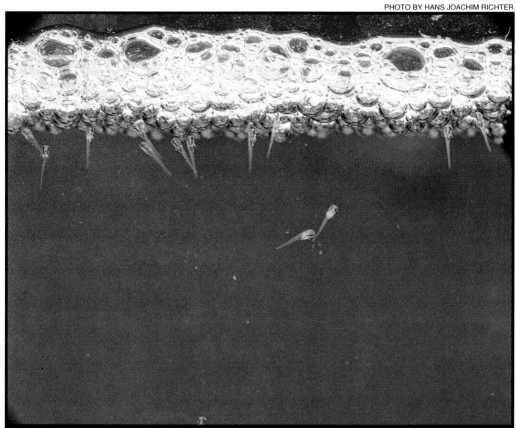

The fry hatching in the nest and beginning to try to leave the nest. The male usually catches them and spits them back into the bubble nest.

begin to assume a horizontal swimming stance. On the day after this, they are capable of swimming about slowly. The male's duties now have been completed. He should be removed. His parental obligation fulfilled, he is likely to consider the fry not his offspring, but his food. Like the female, he should be well fed and housed in clean water. Unlike the female, he will be ready for spawning again in a few days.

Feeding the young

As soon as the fry start swimming, they will start to look for food, so have it ready for them. From this point on you alone are responsible for raising the young successfully. Up to now, the male betta has done most of the work. It is your turn to take over.

The baby bettas will want living food. It must be of a size that can be swallowed easily — almost microscopic. This means infusoria. These are a variety of tiny organisms which thrive in water. Perhaps you will remember them from your high school days as protozoa, paramecia, or rotifers. All abound in stagnant water.

Perhaps you have such a stagnant pool in your vicinity where you can collect infusoria. If not, you will have to culture your own. Tablets for this are available at aquarium shops or you can make your own culture with an infusion of hay, chopped lettuce, or dried lima beans in a large jar of stagnant aquarium water.

When feeding infusoria, always make sure that there are a great many of them in the culture. When culturing them, the first growth in the jar will consist of tremendous quantities of bacteria as well as mold from the dead plant surfaces. The water in this first stage will be very cloudy. It becomes less cloudy when protozoa are present in great numbers. They can be removed by the use of a medicine dropper or rubber bulb syringe, such as those sold for babies. A rubber bulb of the type used for starting filters, with a

A male betta guarding his newly hatched fry.

PHOTO BY HANS JOACHIM RICHTER.

length of rigid plastic tubing attached, can be used also. Draw the infusoria from areas in the jar that have clouds of them visible.

The hatchlings cannot eat baby brine shrimp until they are about a week old. Hard-boiled egg yolk must be fed, a small amount at a time, at least three times a day. Since infusoria are alive and dispersed through the water, enough can be fed in the morning to last all day. Do not foul the water with excess food.

If fed live food, the sexes will be distinguishable as soon as the fish are about two months old. Young bettas cannot be sexed when very young. Even at an early age, however, careful observation will reveal when the anal fins of some begin to grow longer than those of others. The tail and dorsal soon follow suit. Separate the young males as soon as they are recognized to prevent their scrapping with one another. If the space is limited, now is the time to select the best (usually the earliest developers) and dispose of the others.

PHOTO BY HANS JOACHIM RICHTER.

The nest is gone, the fry are spreading out and the male's job is done, so remove him.

Aeration is not advisable in the breeding tank. It may destroy the bubblenest. Once the young are free-swimming, aeration can begin, as it takes several days for the labyrinth to develop sufficiently for the fry to utilize atmospheric oxygen. If the room is cool or dry, keep a glass cover over the tank. A 15-gallon tank is the smallest size you should use to raise an entire spawning. If a tank of at least this size is not available, discard part of the spawn. This sacrifice will permit the remainder to develop properly.

To sum up, then, the major problems are the need for higher temperature, the possibility of severe damage to a reluctant female, the size of the young, and the need for early separation of the males as well as the space in which to isolate them. The color of the prospective parents is of consequence only if one wishes to breed a pure line of a particular color. Since most bettas offered for sale are color hybrids, it is almost impossible to predict the color of their young.

PHOTOS AND FISH BY TANAKA.

Tanaka raised many fish with the gold or Cambodian color. He then experimented with different fin shapes, especially the tail fin. His best varieties are those shown here where the butterfly pattern is so apparent. The butterfly pattern is where the color closest to the body is lighter than that decorating the tips of the fins.

MASS PRODUCTION

Bettas are always in great demand. Many professional breeders raise thousands every year, but are still short of saleable stock. Today, the number of commercial breeders is dwindling because of foreign competition. From overseas, particularly the Far East, bettas are being imported at prices which discourage U.S. breeders from competing. Breeding bettas is a time-consuming process. The professional techniques

PHOTO COURTESY OF DR. HERBERT R. AXELROD.

Orville Tutwiler, the inventor of the butterfly betta in his betta hatchery in Florida in 1955.

Each must have his jar washed and refilled many times during this growth. Each must be packaged for sale. Work trebles for the hatchery which mass-produce bettas. Because of intense competition, the price they bring has dropped as much as 50%, while the breeder's labor and food costs have risen that much, if not more.

Many of today's bettas, imported from overseas, reflect the indiscriminate selection of breeding stock. There vary little from what has been outlined. The chief difference is that, instead of the hobbyist's one breeding tank, the professional devotes whole buildings to rearing thousands of male bettas each in its own glass bowl. Each individual male must be fed every day. is no such thing as breeding a similarly colored male and female to acquire anything like a true strain. Besides a complex color differential, these bettas often carry other unwanted traits, such as short or deformed fins and thick, blunt bodies.

Tanaka refers to these strains as his *blue strains*. They have differing tail fin shapes and different kinds of blue coloration.

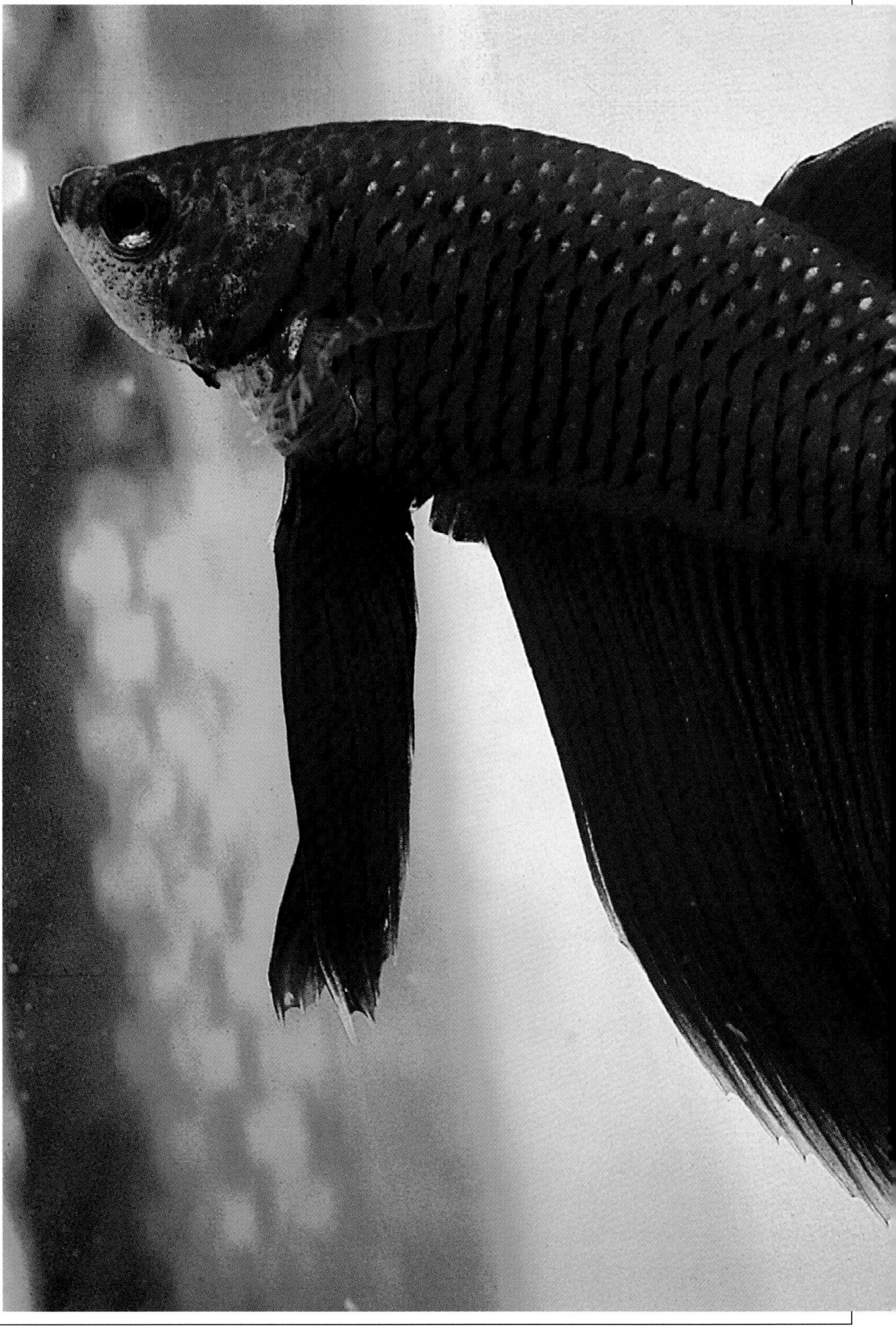

This 1958 champion has yet to be matched in terms of the length of the fins compared to the length of the body. The betta's body has to be strong enough to carry these long fins.

PHOTO BY ANDRE ROTH

PHOTOS AND FISH BY TANAKA.

Not all of Tanaka's breeding efforts are exciting and saleable fish. The photos on this page show the unsuccessful varieties which never made a market niche.

SHOW STANDARDS AND BETTA COMPETITIONS

Betta breeders, like dog owners, flower growers, or cake bakers, like to display their creative efforts in competitive shows. The Siamese fighting fish easily makes a place for itself in any organized fish show. He is put in a class by himself, for what other fish possibly could compete with him?

Rules governing these competitions never have become standardized. This is unfortunate. Not only is the judging more difficult, but the winners' prize traits have meaning only in respect to that particular competition.

What really makes a winning show fish? What do judges look for?

1. The betta should be healthy and have an alert stance. Even when resting, he should seem ready to take off at an adversary.
2. He should have a positive, distinct coloration. There should be no wishy-washy, indefinite hues which only hint at a true color.
3. Finnage should be above average. This is a "show" fish. When spread, the fins should be unmarred and well-formed. There should be no bent rays or crinkled edges. Fin length and size, along with brilliant coloration, are prime requisites. Each should be proportioned to the other so as to create the image of an ideal betta. Having one trait that is subnormal, for instance, a short tail but otherwise lovely finnage and color, is a definite handicap against winning maximum points.

The author, who has judged a countless number of betta shows, feels that a point system for the fighters could be simplicity itself. Points could be awarded as follows:

Color (clarity)	**40**
Fins and Body	**40**
Deportment	**20**
	= 100

One fish should constitute an entry. Bettas should be judged by natural or incandescent light only. The crux on showing is competent, authoritative judges — ones who know what a good betta looks like and can mentally deduct points for any deficiency.

When a betta show has sufficient entrants, sub-classes (usually arranged by color) are established. Occasionally, there is a class for female bettas, but too often this important category is either

In May, 1968 this fish won top prize because of its magnificent color and the strength of its body proportions.

PHOTO BY ANDRE ROTH.

PHOTOS AND FISH BY TANAKA.

The Butterfly Story: (1) true butterflies with the light color in the unpaired fins closest to the body, while the outer edges have intense color; (2) the valueless reverse of the butterfly where the strong color is next to the body; (3) the almost-butterfly; (4) not quite the true butterfly; (5) black splashed so-called butterfly; (6) incomplete butterfly, but beautiful anyway; (7) rare blue-splashed butterfly; (8) the ultimate black splash butterfly.

forgotten or purposely overlooked in favor of the flamboyant male.

Show fish should be presented in flat-sided containers to prevent distortion. Sand, plants, or ornaments are unnecessary except to serve the esthetic senses.

The albino fighting fish

In 1953, the aquarium hobby received a slight jolt when the author of this book reported the finding of a true pink-eyed male albino betta. It appeared among his stock, as many albinos do, by sheer accident. Thought at first to be a very pale specimen of the Cambodian type of betta, close inspection revealed the unnatural eyes and its true distinction. Naturally, it was given every consideration.

Only once before, in 1927, had such an albino been reported. This was by the veteran German aquarist Wilhelm Schreitmuller in Leipzig. He noticed it in a tank of tropical fish in the store of Herr W. Glaschter. With typical albino weakness, the German betta lived only a short time. It was preserved and presented to the Magdeburger Museum. It never was bred.

The one found in 1953, in spite of having difficulty seeing and an aversion to bright light, prospered and became robust. Three unsuccessful attempts were made to breed him in the normal manner. In spite of

building a fine nest, he could not see the female unless she was directly in front of his nose. Because of this, his courting activities gradually dwindled.

Then a special breeding setup was attempted. It proved successful. The pair was confined together by means of

PHOTO BY GENE WOLFSHEIMER.

The albino male raised by the author. The photo is 40 years old!

a piece of glass in a small space with scarcely ten square inches of surface. Here the female could hardly escape his view. The courtship and eventual spawning were a success. Then it was discovered that the albino had no desire to care for the eggs. The nest broke up and scattered. The eggs dropped to the bottom unattended and went bad. Obviously, some other procedure was in order.

Once again the breeders were introduced into their limited confines. A second spawning ensued. As soon as it was completed, a three-inch laboratory Petri dish was slipped under the nest. It entrapped both eggs and the nest, and maintained but a fractional depth of water. This time most of the eggs survived. A small spawning of about fifty fry was reared.

The fry started to color when they were about five-eighths of an inch long. All were of a bluish-purple color. No hoped-for albinos were to be seen. This was expected. Albinism is a recessive characteristic. For the young to show it, the genes must be present in both parents. By the time these young had grown to breeding maturity, the male albino had perished, so a daughter could not be spawned back to him. As expected, brother-to-sister matings never resulted in another albino.

There are many red-eyed bettas which appear from time to time but they are never inbred because of their limited commercial appeal.

PHOTO BY TANAKA.

PHOTOS AND FISH BY TANAKA.

Weird tail shapes: (1) common split tail; (2) double split tail; (3) lyre tail; (4) wild tail; (5) ragged tail; (6) 4 pointed or double split tail; (7) upper sword tail; (8) pinch tail which never opens.

PHOTOS AND FISH BY TANAKA.

Perhaps one of Tanaka's greatest developments has been the intensification of the blue pigment, even in Cambodiam Bettas. Here are examples of the blue intruding pleasantly onto the Cambodia color.

PHOTO BY TANAKA.

One of Tanaka's albino bettas. This is a female.

What had happened? Just one mistake and the albino betta again disappeared from the hobby. Thinking that the albino male had come from my light-bodied Cambodian stock, a beautiful light-bodied female had been provided for the spawnings. Had the albino been derived from this stock, the offspring should have been of the Cambodian strain, also. Instead, the result was dark-colored offspring.

The results of future brother-to-sister matings should have been predictable on theoretical grounds. From each sixteen offspring, there should have appeared nine wild or dark-colored bettas, three Cambodian light-bodied fish, and four albinos.

There did appear mixed spawnings of light and dark specimens. However, the eye-straining inspections failed to turn up another albino. Then Tanaka did it in 1994!

Decorative items work well in the betta tank because fishes often like to hide from the sometimes aggressive Siamese fighter. Your pet shop should have several products to show you.

PHOTO BY BLUE RIBBON PET PRODUCTS.

INDEX